Up, Up and Away

CENTRAL SCOTLAND

Edited by Sarah Andrew

First published in Great Britain in 2000 by
YOUNG WRITERS
Remus House,
Coltsfoot Drive,
Peterborough, PE2 9JX
Telephone (01733) 890066

Copyright Contributors 2000

HB ISBN 0 75432 182 7
SB ISBN 0 75432 183 5

FOREWORD

This year, the Young Writers' Up, Up & Away competition proudly presents a showcase of the best poetic talent from over 70,000 up-and-coming writers nationwide.

Successful in continuing our aim of promoting writing and creativity in children, our regional anthologies give a vivid insight into the thoughts, emotions and experiences of today's younger generation, displaying their inventive writing in its originality.

The thought, effort, imagination and hard work put into each poem impressed us all and again the task of editing proved challenging due to the quality of entries received, but was nevertheless enjoyable. We hope you are as pleased as we are with the final selection and that you continue to enjoy *Up, Up & Away Central Scotland* for many years to come.

CONTENTS

St Andrew's Primary School, Falkirk

Shieldhill Primary School

The Poems

MY MAGIC CARPET

Flying on my magic carpet,
Soaring through the never-ending, light-blue sky.
Miniature commas staring up at me,
Looping the loop,
With the powerful wind pulling back my face.

Flying on my magic carpet,
Along the withered plains of Africa.
Dung makes its way through the calming air,
Not a care in the world at all.
Until the roaring of a massive wildebeest stampede comes crashing by.

Flying on my magic carpet,
Miraculous view above the booming deep blue sea.
Thrilled to see a great whale splashing about,
A sparkling fish slide,
With weeds hanging from it.

Flying on my magic carpet,
Ambling along the different coloured fields.
Like a huge patterned quilt,
Amazed to see a seagull passing by.
Mixed emotions as I fly for home.

Getting off my magic carpet,
Feeling light-headed and peelie-wally.
Felt like an electrical bird that wouldn't stop,
Could still hear the mumbling of the wind.
Can't wait to be on my magic carpet again.

Laura Smith (10)
Antonine Primary School

THE PARACHUTE

As the wind blows rapidly in my face
I am trembling with fear
The world looks like a patchwork quilt
Flashing by my eyes
I feel like I just burst and I am
Flying to and fro
I hear an incredible noise
Rushing past my ears
Then I start descending
Every second of the way
I'm getting closer
And it's getting faster then . . .
Bang!
I reach the ground all in one piece.

Rebecca Smith (10)
Antonine Primary School

COLOURS

Blue is for the sky, ocean, or the sea,
Blue for Saltire, and the cold for me.
Restless seas splish, splash off the cliffs,
Summer skies such a clear, clear blue.

A stream of blood in a blazing fire,
Strawberries ripe and ready to eat.
Raspberries round, juicy and squishy,
Fire so hot and glazed.

Yellow is the sun, daffodils, daisies,
Or romantic candlelight at dinner.
As the sun dries up the seas so blue,
Sunflowers growing to be tall in the spring breeze.

Black, black, horrible black is the blackest cat,
Or the black coal for the blazing fire.
The sky at night is black, with a sprinkle of sugar on it,
The wicked witch's pointed hat is black.

Adele Hamilton (10)
Antonine Primary School

SOARING THROUGH THE SKY

I am soaring through the skies like a bird rapidly approaching freedom
Like the world is my oyster
People look like ants
Cars look like beetles
The exquisite sunset straight ahead
Clouds like marshmallows floating
The luxuriously colossal blue sky
I start to descend
Fresh air hitting my face
I never want to land although I know I have to
Soon my great flight will have to end
I can hear birds chirping
Swerving down to land
I know tomorrow I am going up, up and away again.

Sian Black (10)
Antonine Primary School

MAGICAL CARPET

Up in the sky wind blows in my face as we go faster and faster.
Birds singing sweet songs of happiness.
Swerving round corners as fast as the speed of light.
Children laughing and having fun.
Lambs bobbing about with fleeces as white as snow.
It feels like I am floating on water.
I feel as light as a feather as I soar through the sky.

Forress Smith (10)
Antonine Primary School

UP, UP, IN AN AEROPLANE

Forced back in your chair like someone has pushed you
Cars look like beetles
People are just lines
Houses are squares
I feel sick when I look down
I can hear something humming
Hmmmm a-hmmmm a-hmmmm
The engine making a noise
Fasten your seatbelts, we're about to land
Eeeeekkk the brakes are slowing down
Phew! I'm glad that's over.

Alyson Farrell (10)
Antonine Primary School

THE BIG BALLOON

When the burner goes on
It's like red, yellow and orange fire
Going high up in flames.

Everything looked so microscopic
Horses like tiny black dots
And little sheep like fluffy bits of cotton wool.

The balloon was swerving from side to side
Up in the freezing cold blue sky
The rushing ice-cold wind goes quickly by my face.

I hear the whistle of the wind getting slower and slower as I go down
I land in a huge field where I hear the birds sing
When I hit the bottom I get a whiff of the fresh green grass.

Lauren Rae (11)
Antonine Primary School

AS I GLIDE

As I glide through the fresh air on my colourful magic carpet,
The wind dashes by my ears like a tornado,
When I look down, it's like my room - a wicked mess.

As I glide through the fresh air on my colourful magic carpet,
I float above ants and matchboxes,
When I drift past a beehive I smell lovely sticky honey.

As I glide through the fresh air on my colourful magic carpet,
When I float down to earth I feel wonderful,
It would be superb to be back in the peaceful snowy sky.

Amy Clark (10)
Antonine Primary School

BUNGEE JUMP

Today's the day for the bungee jump,
Up, up and away in the helicopter,
Ready to jump 200ft from the sky above.
Waiting to take off, it was terrifying,
I closed my eyes and I was away,
My stomach had left me hanging there,
Upside down I was trembling,
The waves were getting rougher and rougher,
As if it was angry,
I was getting dizzy and scared,
At last it came to a stop,
And it left me hanging there.

Stacey Alexander (10)
Antonine Primary School

WHEN I'M FLYING

When I look down I see houses like boxes
The buildings look like rooms
Roads look like rivers
Grass looks like a sheet of paper
The gardens look like a drawing.

The vertical noise gets louder and louder as we get closer
The aeroplane's engine is really noisy
When you listen to the wind, it is really wild.

When you first get into the plane
You feel excited about going on holiday
When you are in the air
You just feel sick
It is terrifying when you're really high in the sky.

Stuart Stephens (10)
Antonine Primary School

THE GLIDER

I remember when I was on a glider
Up very high in the sky
Where it is so quiet and gentle.

When you are 100 feet in the air
There are no buses and lorries
To toot and annoy you.

But every time you take a breath
You taste something horrible
Like cold chips and rotten eggs.

When I look down I can see the lake
With the ducks looking like dots
And the island looking the shape of a rubber.

Scott Bain (10)
Antonine Primary School

COLOURS OF THE WORLD

X-Pac wears bright green trousers when he's fighting in the ring.
Blood is red and sticky when it's pouring from my head.
The night sky is black when the beautiful sun goes down.
Sandy beaches are yellow when I'm on my holidays.
Huge, fluffy clouds are white when they move across the sky.
The beautiful sea is blue when I swim in it.

James O'Brien (10)
Antonine Primary School

ALIENS

Bruno went bananas when
He saw my pink pyjamas
And told about the aliens
Last night.

He said I smelt cheesy and
Looked very wheezy while taking
A bite of a kite.

He said I was bright
And had very good sight
But when it comes to aliens
I don't.

He still wouldn't believe me
And said it was easy
So he might let me off
This time.

Jenna Clark (10)
Beaconhurst School

CHICKEN

Chicken, chicken, chicken,
Is my favourite food,
It's tasty and delicious,
And very good to chew.
The butcher sells it in his shop
Every single day,
And you can bet me anything,
You'll see me there each day.

Fiona Menzies (10)
Beaconhurst School

ANIMALS

Animals skip, animals hop
You buy animals in a pet shop.
Animals jump, animals flop
Animals all around the shop.

Animals squeak, animals squawk
Animals, they are a noisy lot.
With long necks, with short legs, fat and thin
Up above in the trees and down under the seas.

Animals in the jungle
Animals in the sea.
Animals in our houses
Just like you and me.

Nichola Heron (10)
Beaconhurst School

MY GUINEA PIG

My guinea pig sits in his cage and waits.

Three hours go by
And he is still
Waiting.

The birds sing and
His best friend squeaks
But still he is waiting.

And then the lock flies open
And there stand I
He gives out the loudest squeak.

I run over and give him
The biggest carrot ever!

Joanna Sandilands (10)
Beaconhurst School

THE HORSE'S PROMISE

Where you want me to go I'll go
Even though I will not know
Whether I'm going to a hack or show
As I promised I will go.

If it's a show when we arrive
You take me through my paces and make me alive
Then we jump when the bell goes *ding*
Or do dressage in a small ring.

Sometimes we go endurance riding
Which is over a long distance
Sometimes my rider shows resistance
But we keep going on and on
Till the finish line we come upon.

If we go on a hack
Then we usually follow a track
We may go for a short or maybe a long
But my rider usually sings a silly song.

When we are home again
I am glad she is mine
Because the two of us are best friends
And that's the bottom line.

Louise Lumsden (10)
Beaconhurst School

THE EAGLE

The eagle flies in the stormy sky
Searching for his prey
He swoops down close to the ground
What will he find today?

With a sweep and a plunge
He drops like a stone
His talons outstretched
But his prey has gone.

He flies away so sad, so sad
But some tiny creature is very glad
Back in its home cosy and warm
Far away from the winter storm

The screech of the eagle
Still lingers on.

Gillian Stewart (10)
Beaconhurst School

HARRI

Big brown eyes
Big brown paws
Big brown legs
And big brown jaws

A shiny coat
And shiny eyes
She loves to greet me
When I rise

Have you guessed
What this is about?
It's about my dog Harri
From Dalmally!

Scott Ferguson (10)
Beaconhurst School

CRICKET

Cricket is a lovely game
I really like to play it,
Someday I hope I'll be the same
As my hero Mark Alleyn.
They play it here,
They play it there,
All round the world and everywhere,
Africa, India, Pakistan too
Australia, Zimbabwe and Timbuktu.
Batters, bowlers and fielders play
And umpires are there to save the day.

Richard Carswell (10)
Beaconhurst School

THE GIANT

Giant, giant, so big and tall
Why is it that I am so small?

Your big, long arms
And clumpy feet, and mine
Are oh so petite!

With lumpy nose and baldy head,
You've grown too big for your bed!

Even though you're so tall,
The bigger you are the harder you fall!

Danielle McRorie-Smith (10)
Beaconhurst School

THE RUGBY TEAM

There once was a rugby team, they were really mean
Fatso, Skinny, Plugger, Rugger, Tiny,
Little Johnny, Rudolph, Smuggler
Kicking, slapping, throwing, punching
They were the people to do the crunchin'

One fine Saturday they quickly went
Down to the rugby pitch smelling the winning scent
Played really tough
As usual really rough
And won the game!

They went back to the change rooms
Really, really happy
They even told their guard dog Slappy!

Then they celebrated all that night
Still being the only team
To put up a good fight.

Matthew Haywood (10)
Beaconhurst School

MY DOGS

A woof here and a woof there
That is my dogs - Crosby and Hobbes.
They woof everybody up in the morning
Except me! Because I am too sleepy.
They gulp anything down
With a right good will
And want anything more.
They have sparks flying from their paws
When they go to the vets
But they always get a treat.

Jonathan Campbell (10)
Beaconhurst School

HUGE ELFY

When I was sitting at the table
All by myself,
Along comes an elf,
'Who are you?'
'I'm just a huge fat elf'
'I'm not surprised,
You're just as big as the room!'
'I can't fit into a car
Brooom! Brooom!'
'Where do you live?'
'Merlin Magic Magician Land'
'Wow! That's lovely!
Bye bye huge elfy.'

Sheena Cheema (9)
Beaconhurst School

THE ALIEN

An alien came from outer space,
He was not of the human race,
He was a massive size,
And had great big eyes,
And a huge big wrinkly face.

This alien's name was Mr Boon,
He lived in a helium balloon,
One day it popped
And he flew all the way to the moon.

He landed hard and broke a limb,
It was so sore he felt grim,
His head fell off
When he started to cough,
And that was the end of him.

Andrew Mackay (10)
Beaconhurst School

UP AND AWAY BUTTERFLY

Have you seen a butterfly
Fly up into the sky?
Yes, that little butterfly
Flying behind that tree
Flying, fluttering into the sky
Away it floats
Butterfly, oh how I wish
I could go with you.

David Robertson (10)
Beaconhurst School

FIERY MOUNTAIN

Below the Earth's crust
The magma is sitting so peacefully in the mantle
As if waiting for the perfect moment.
A small town called Terhazza has no idea of the trauma ahead.

The magma decides the time has come to give them nightmares
for the rest of their lives.
It rushes up the vent as if in a relay race
Ready to pass the molten baton to the unsuspecting people below.
Ash, rocks and debris shoot thousands of metres into the air.
People turn from whatever they are doing.
The market goes silent for a few seconds, then panic is in the air.
Debris comes descending, lance-like, at tremendous speed towards
the Earth.
People run for cover when they should be running for their lives.
Ash and rock distract the villagers as the lava creeps up behind them,
turning when they hear an explosion.
People freeze as the boiling lava paves a path of destruction.
It crawls and climbs over the scrambling villagers.

Alan McCluskey (10)
Cambusbarron Primary School

COLD DAY

The frost changes everything it meets.
It turns dogs white like polar bears.
The town seems like a winter wonderland
with a glow beaming down on the snow-capped hill.
The snow tumbles from a great tree.

Children disturb the tranquillity,
Making snowmen,
Throwing snowballs,
Sledging in a frosted heaven.
Winter is here.

Joe Kelly (11)
Cambusbarron Primary School

FAILURE/SUCCESS

Failure is a dark tunnel
Which has no ending
Like an earthquake
Which snakes the world.

Success is a bridge
Sturdy and safe
Like a wind
Blowing smoothly.

Kenneth Broadfoot (11)
Cambusbarron Primary School

A SNOWY DAY

The thick snow lies like a quilt over the cold ground.
It lies with no footprints except that of a bird.
Children wrapped up tight
Build snowmen with numb hands,
Then go into their homes,
One by one,
For mugs of steaming hot chocolate.
Slowly, more people emerge
To clear snow from their paths.

Icicles hanging from a frozen roof
Sway gently in the wind
As the snow falls again.
Flake by flake
It covers cleared paths
Putting snowmen to sleep
Until children come again.

Shona MacLeod (11)
Cambusbarron Primary School

THE ANDES

High in the mountains
A trickling stream tiptoes so slowly
You hardly know its moving.

High in the mountains
The Quechua live
Wearing ponchos to keep them warm.

Lynne Blore (10)
Cambusbarron Primary School

A SNOWY DAY

Snow covers everything in its path.
Rooftops have fluffy hats.
Gutters wear icicle jewellery
And windows steam up with condensation.

Kids have snowball fights
And race down snow-covered slopes.
My plump snowman sits in the garden
Watching everything I do.

Diana McLaren (11)
Cambusbarron Primary School

TWELVE O'CLOCK

The clock is ticking
The hands are moving
It's twelve o'clock
What can I do?
The rain is drip dropping
Lightning and thunder are coming
I cannot get to sleep
It's too noisy
I hide under the pillow
And go to sleep.

Kitty Ho (9)
Denny Primary School

MY PET

My pet is a good friend,
He's as fast as a jet,
And yet he is friendly,
And very playful.

He cheers me up
When I am sad
And licks me
And jumps on me.

My pet is a good friend,
I like him
And he likes me.
I would like to say
We are good friends.

Jennifer Willgerod (10)
Denny Primary School

THE GUY WHO LIVES DOWN OUR STREET

The guy who lives down our street has
very, very smelly feet,
and if you look at them far or near,
your eyes will bring many a tear.

And when he goes to the shop down our street,
this guy with the very, very smelly feet,
straightaway he knocks out the guy at the till,
so that he doesn't have to pay a single bill.

When he comes to your own house,
he knocks out your pet mouse.
A terrible terror with his smelly feet,
that's the guy who lives down our street.

Martin Philip McPherson (9)
Denny Primary School

THAT RABBIT!

I had a very cheeky rabbit
Who always made me feel crabbit.
One day I took her in for exercise,
And she went to the kitchen and ate three pies.
So I tried to put her in her cage
But she just started a rage
And bit a hole in my finger.

When I finally got her in her cage,
I read my book, but when I turned the page,
A little white head popped out.
Oh, what a little snout,
My sister had let her out again!

Julie Love (9)
Denny Primary School

RAIN

Rain is falling heavily down
Rain is *splashing* as it hits the ground.
Rain makes me feel very sad
Rain makes today very bad.

Rain keeps me in all day long
Rain makes me cry all day.
Rain still tumbling down the gutter
Rain still pouring down outside.
Rain! Rain! Rain!

Victoria McDonald (9)
Denny Primary School

RAIN

Rain, rain is pouring down,
It's making lots of puddles,
Rain, rain is pouring down,
It's making lots of muddles.
At first it's just dripping,
But soon it is tipping,
It starts to patter loudly
And then it gets cloudy.
Soon comes a storm,
But I'm inside nice and warm.

Nicola McEwan (9)
Denny Primary School

WEATHER

Today it's Friday and it's raining
Out in the rain it's like a pool
But I can't swim in it, I have school.
Monday it was sunny,
I was hot and sweaty
With my school clothes on.
On Tuesday I didn't watch the weather forecast
But I got caught in the hailstones;
I was sore from them hitting me.
Wednesday it was thundering and lightning;
I didn't go to school
Because it was so bad.
At last it's half-past three.
The rain is still forming huge pools;
Now I can swim in them.
Hurrah!

Amy Tennant (9)
Denny Primary School

WHEN I AM HAPPY

On Monday afternoon I played with my friends at the park
This made me happy.

On Tuesday evening I sat on my mum's knee
This made me really happy.

On Wednesday afternoon I went shopping with my gran
This made me very happy.

On Thursday afternoon I walked my dog with my sister
This made me extremely happy.

On Friday evening I went to my dad's house
This made me happy, happy, happy.

Bethan Neilson (10)
Denny Primary School

YUM, YUM, FOR MY TUM

Eyeballs and ears,
Toes and hearts,
All sorts of bugs.
My favourite is children's bones
And for afters, heart pie
Because I am a witch
And all of these are
Yum, yum, for my tum!

Henry Bennie (9)
Denny Primary School

FRUIT

Round, green or purple
Small, not big
Tastes nice and juicy -
It's a grape.

Red and round
Little seeds all over
Quite big, nice and juicy -
It's a strawberry.

Orange and round
Little white seeds
You have to peel it -
It's an orange.

Red is for strawberries
Orange is for oranges
Yellow is for bananas or lemons
Green is for grapes.

Fiona McKay (9)
Denny Primary School

GO TO SLEEP PETE!

'For the tenth time, Pete please go to sleep!'
'I can't.'
'Well, think about that cat you saw on the mat,
Or the rice you thought was ever so nice,
Or a holiday abroad, it would be ever so nice.'
'Okay Dad, goodnight and thanks for the tip-top advice.'

Emma Bryder (9)
Denny Primary School

I'M BORED

When I'm stuck inside and it's raining
When I've got nobody to play with
When I'm sitting in the classroom listening
When I'm travelling in the car to school
Oh boy! I'm bored.

When I'm bored my pet always cheers me up
When I'm bored I can just play some games
When I'm bored I can go and draw a picture
When I'm bored I can go and surf the internet
I can do all these things when I'm bored.

Scott Cowan (10)
Denny Primary School

HIGH IN THE SKY

I can go high in the sky
I fly way up high
I can go higher than high
I can go way down low
That's how far I can go.

Up in the clouds
Up in the sky
Over the hills
Underground
That's how much I have found.

Emma Maxwell (10)
Denny Primary School

MONSTERS

Monsters yellow red and green
the kind you have never seen
On their heads are golden horns
and curly wurly hair
others have twisted knees
They may think they're beautiful
but really look like carrots and peas
Some have really spiky backs
that make you go *wee* to the moon and back
All safe you feel tucked up at night
until a bed bug gives you a fright
But don't be afraid he's only hungry
and anything will do
A piece of skin, a crumb of toast
or maybe even a Sunday roast
So don't be scared if you feel a tug
its only a tiny bed bug.

Jamie-Lee Green (9)
East Plean Primary School

BABIES

Rosy cheeks,
Big eyes,
Little limbs,
Often cries.

Grows fast,
Very small,
Big smile,
They learn to crawl.

Easily hurt,
Little bundles of joy,
Could be a girl,
Could be a boy.

Cute, aren't they?

Victoria Scruton (11)
Knoxland Primary School

THE CAR

T   is for troublesome when the car will not start
H   is for hazards when I am trying to park
E   is for engine that turns with a spark

C   is for congestion on all of the roads
A   is for anger at the road hog behind
R   is for the radio soothing my mind.

Craig Brown (11)
Knoxland Primary School

FISH

Keeping fish is Alan's hobby
His favourite fish is called Robbie
He has a shark that eats the rest
I bet that he thinks he's the best.

He keeps the fish tank very clean
And all the plants are coloured green
You have to keep the water hot
Or else the fish will die a lot.

Above the tank there is a light
That keeps the colours nice and bright
We give them flakes for their food
'Cause it puts them in a happy mood.

My favourite has a red, red nose
And in the dark it often glows
The other fish are often found
Following him round and round
He shows the way to all the rest
And that is why I like him best.

David Ferguson (11)
Knoxland Primary School

MY FAMILY

My dad is in the police
He sits and has a feast
My mum works in a school
They think she's really cool
My sister's in the Academy
They say she's a real baddie
My brother's in P3
He thinks it is as good as can be
While I'm in Primary 7
They think I'll go to heaven.

Robert Stewart (11)
Knoxland Primary School

SASHA

I love my cat
My cat loves me
When I am at school
She looks for me.

I give her treats
She purrs at me
This is how I like it to be.

She is the best
I know she is
At bedtime
I give her a kiss.

Claire McKinley (11)
Knoxland Primary School

THINK OF OTHERS

Think how you feel when people starve
You must feel upset
Knowing people die every day
Because they're hungry.

Knowing you come home to food on the table
While people eat crumbs and drink little
You know you can buy food when it runs out
Others are not so lucky.

Instead of wasting money on treats
You could give some to charity
Because people are starving and dying
Instead of yourself, think of others.

Graham Johnston (11)
Knoxland Primary School

CASPER

My big sister's dog Casper,
Every day he gets faster.
Running with me down the park,
And every mile he likes to bark.
He looks like a fine lad,
But inside he's really bad.
He ate the couch, he ate the table,
Now he's on to all the cables.
In the house there's nothing left,
And Laura's put it down to theft.
Andy said 'It wasn't me,
I only ate the Christmas tree.'
Between the two Laura's heart is broke,
But I only wrote this for a joke.

Gordon Caldwell (11)
Knoxland Primary School

THE FOUR SEASONS POEM

The winter has gone,
And spring is here,
Trees will have buds,
The sky will come clear.
March winds will blow,
And melt will the snow,
Birds soon will sing,
And Easter bells will ring.
Seeds can be sown into the ground,
In the trees birds' nests can be found,
When the flowers bloom and the birds start to sing,
Then we will know it's the end of spring.
Now spring has gone and colours appear,
Red, blue and greens are now here,
Out comes the sun, away goes the rain,
Here we are till summer again.
Then it all starts, the leaves start to flutter,
Rain comes down into the gutter,
The whites of frost they appear,
The shades of autumn disappear.

Pamela Allen (11)
Knoxland Primary School

THE PEACE DEAL

In Northern Ireland everybody shoots,
They're all trying to sign the books.
All the groups say things violently,
Politicians do it quietly.
Groups hand over some of their weapons,
And the news reports indiscretion.

Jonathan Smith (12)
Knoxland Primary School

SPIDER

A spider with its great long legs
It is so light, as light as a feather
It weaves a web to catch some flies
It catches four and wants more.

It likes to wait for me to come
It catches one more and goes to sleep
The spider is full of joy and glee
But just then it catches a bee.

Jonathan Benson (10)
Knoxland Primary School

WAR

War is hell, like killing someone
What would you do?
Scream
Shout
Or fight?
They fought for us, they died for us
They did everything that they
Could do
Some fought
Some just waited in the corner
Waiting to *die*
At least we are still here
Thanks to them.

James Young (11)
Knoxland Primary School

KATIE

Katie is my rabbit
Loving her's a habit
She's black, not white
She cannot write
She has long ears
She has no tears
She wears no clothes
Because everybody knows
Katie is my rabbit.

Emma Grindlay (11)
Knoxland Primary School

FRIENDS

Friends are people who always care
Friends are people who are always there
Friends are people who have the time
Friends are people who are always kind.

Paula Wiggins (11)
Knoxland Primary School

WINNIE THE POOH

Winnie the Pooh is a loveable bear
He is cute and cuddly and very fair
He has a gift, a heart of gold
So many friends, young and old
He has a house in Hundred Acre Wood
He would eat honey every day if he could.

Carly McGrath (11)
Knoxland Primary School

ZOMBIES

Daylight fades as night draws near
The shadows grow, the people fear.
Grovelling, groaning from the graves
Humans are their living slaves.

They come at night their fear to spread
The walking, stalking, living dead
Your blood runs cold, you hold your breath
Praying you won't meet your death.

Rotting flesh, dismembered limbs
Good Christian folk recite their hymns
They'll suck your blood and eat your brain
Once you're dead, you'll feel no pain.

As daylight dawns, they must retreat
The sunlight comes, they feel the heat
Back to their icy lairs they sway
They can't be seen by light of day.

Relief is clear for all to share
Returned from trembling and despair
The shadows fade, they're gone from sight
Will they come back another night?

Lewis Hutchison (11)
Knoxland Primary School

MAD SHOPPER

My mum is a mad shopper
I think she is off her trolley
She buys lots of sweets
And for my sister a little dolly
She grabs everything from the aisle
Shopping with her may take a while

She always complains there is nothing to eat
So that's another walk down the street
She shops and shops and shops some more
She is the last person out of Safeway's door.

Jennifer Connolly (11)
Knoxland Primary School

MY CAT

I have a cat
It caught a rat
I hit it over the head with a
Baseball bat
It's got a bump on its head
And now it's dead
So *ha ha* ratty
I'll go for a bird next time instead.

David McAllister (11)
Knoxland Primary School

IN MY ROOM

In my house my room is so scary
There is a ghost in my room called Mary
I hear some noises under my bed
Sometimes they come up right over my head.

In my wardrobe I hear some whispers
Maybe it is Mary's bushy whiskers
On my desk my papers flick
It makes me want to really tick.

In the night the wind is howling
But it could never compare to Susy's growling
Back to the ghost in my room
I think she should go back to her tomb.

Gayle Hindle (11)
Knoxland Primary School

GOLDFISH

Sometimes I wonder how boring it is
To be a goldfish.
Just swimming around and round their
Tank all day.
And do they have names other than
The ones we give them?
Do they have families
Can they speak to each other?
The answer - only goldfish know.

Lynsey Morrison (11)
Knoxland Primary School

ALL ABOUT ME AND MY FRIEND

I am so brilliant, I am so cool.
I am as tough as a big fat bull.
I can tell jokes, I can do tricks.
I can juggle with my mum's cooking sticks.

Enough about me, let's talk about you.
You make me want to go *boo hoo!*
You are so lucky to have me as a friend.
Now I am coming to the very end.

That is enough about me and my friend.

Amy Burt (11)
Laurieston Primary School

MY BROTHER

Brothers - where would you be without them?
Especially when they're a pain.
I'm talking about *my* brother.
This is the one you should learn.
They jump, kick, punch and sometimes
really annoy you.
Or they can be football crazy, or maybe they're
Too good for you.
I wonder what my brother will be like when he's 42?
He'll probably be at the pub until he's 52!
My brother is annoying
Especially when he doesn't get away with it!

Lauren Mackinlay (11)
Laurieston Primary School

BROTHERS

Who would like a brother
Who thinks he's pretty cool!
But actually he's nothing but a fool
Who's big and fat and the size of a rat.
Now who would like a brother just like that?

Who would like a brother
Who picks his nose
Bites his toes
And gets washed by the garden hose?
Now who would like a brother like that?

Who would like a brother
Who thinks he's all that
And goes greeting till he's more like a pussy cat
Now who would like a brother like that?

Who would like a brother
Who wears geeky glasses,
Fancies all the lassies
And stinks of loads of gases?
Now who would like a brother like that?

But I've got a brother
Who's cool and courageous
And everyone wants a brother like that!

Jillian Fraser (11)
Laurieston Primary School

WHISPERS

'She kissed him.'
'She didn't!'
'She did.'
'Who did?'
'Miss Drew!'
'She wouldn't.'
'She did!'
'Kissed who?'
'Mr Kerr.'
'He shouldn't.'
'He let her.'
'Kissed him where?'
'Over there.'
'What, by the gym?'
'Don't be so dim.'
'By the rubbish skips?'
'No.'
'Well where?'
'Smack on the lips.'
'Oooooooh!'

Nicola Oliver (11)
Laurieston Primary School

MY SISTER

My sister is such a blister.
I just want to fist her.
But when I go to hit her.
Then I slightly miss her.
I'm not supposed to hit her,
But I do it anyway.
Then I get into trouble.
What more can I say?

Louise Colbecki (11)
Laurieston Primary School

PEOPLE

Andrew is big,
Lena is small,
I am medium
And so is Paul.

Marti Jack (11)
Laurieston Primary School

MY TEACHER

What is it my teacher does?
My teacher gives us sums - sometimes too many!
Other times she gives us homework - worksheets to
Do all the time.
She gives people punishments
In fact she's good at that!
I think that she'll all right most of the time.
I like her best just before the holidays.
She let us do anything we want!

Scott Cowan (11)
Laurieston Primary School

PORTRAIT OF A FRIEND

If I had a problem I would go to my friend,
Because she would understand
If I hurt myself I would go to my friend,
Because she would help me
If I want to laugh I would go to my friend,
Because she is very funny
If I need company I would go to my friend,
Because she is really cool,
She is my friend
And I'm glad!

Lori Henderson (10)
Rhu Primary School

PORTRAIT OF A FRIEND

I like my friend, she's really cool
She tells the truth to me
She's honest and caring
And keeps a secret
She understands my problems
And tries to cheer me up
But we like to have a laugh!

Samantha Chew (10)
Rhu Primary School

PORTRAIT OF A FRIEND

My friend is funny,
She likes to laugh,
She is kind, cool and popular,
She likes to make crafts,
Her favourite colour is blue,
She likes her blue bell-bottoms
And her short top T-shirt
With her minibeast earrings.

Heather Wilson (10)
Rhu Primary School

PORTRAIT OF A FRIEND

She's cool and she's funny and she likes to dance,
She gives you all a very big chance,
If you do something wrong or break your head
She'll take you to the office and you'll go to the head.

I'm really, really glad that she's my friend
I'd like to tell you who it is
        It's Heather.

Fiona Campbell (10)
Rhu Primary School

PORTRAIT OF A FRIEND

My friend is helpful,
My friend is kind,
She likes to have a laugh,
She is very friendly too.
My friend likes to play
She has her ears pierced
She is really cool.
My friend has blonde hair
So you'll know her anywhere,
My friend hates fruit
But loves her chocolate
She has cool glasses as well.

Rachel Findlay (10)
Rhu Primary School

PORTRAIT OF A FRIEND

Here she comes walking the street,
Purple jeans on and eating jelly beans.
Her blonde hair bouncing while
She fiddles with her ears,
She looks so cool I wish she would rule.

Becky Balshaw (10)
Rhu Primary School

AUTUMN DAYS

The summer leaves fall off the trees.
The summer sun turns into a gentle breeze.
All you hear is rustling of the squirrels.
Puzzling to get the chestnuts free.
Now the farmers are rushing to get
The crops that are thrushing.
I look outside my window to see the acorns
And potatoes are nearly ready.
The nights go dark, I can't play in the park.
Fruit and raspberries are yummy in people's tummies.
Bonfires are so much fun
But sadly Guy Fawkes was shot with a gun.
Now it's nearly the end and the birds are away with friends.
The colours are red and brown.
The roads are slippy with frost.
But my place is next to the fire because autumn
Is disappearing, bye bye autumn,
It's time for winter.

Craig Costin (11)
Rhu Primary School

AUTUMN

Autumn has arrived,
Summer has gone,
The farmer is really busy,
The crackling of bonfires,
The setting of fireworks is the right season
For Guy Fawkes.

The migrating birds are beautiful,
The temperature drops even more during the night
Fir cones and conkers are fun to collect,
The ripe fruit are good to taste,
While birds are flying south,
The squirrels are collecting conkers and acorns,
For the winter,

The farmers and labourers are threshing the wheat,
For everybody else around,
Animals are getting ready for winter,
It's a lovely season.

Mark Young (11)
Rhu Primary School

AUTUMN

Brown, red, golden leaves falling from the trees,
The temperature drops,
There is also night frost,
Fruit falling from the trees
And also soft brown chestnuts,
That squirrels eat.

Hallowe'en has come again,
You go trick or treating,
With lit up pumpkins,
A bag for the sweets
And also you get money,
If you are very, very lucky.

There is also Guy Fawkes night
Where you can see fireworks that light up,
They look like
Shooting stars!

Natalie Gore (11)
Rhu Primary School

AUTUMN DAYS

Autumn days, they are very dull,
The acorns start to fall and the conkers too,
The animals have gone to hibernate
And the birds are away to somewhere warm,
The leaves start to fall in groups of
Gold, red and brown.

Autumn is nearly over now,
The temperature has dropped and it's really cold,
I want it warm again,
The leaves have all fallen off
On the bonfire the smell of leaves is really rich,
When I fight with my dad, I always win,
Because I boil mine so it's rock hard.

The bonfire's on and it's roasting hot,
Crackle, bang, boom go the acorns on top,
The days are getting darker and very much colder,
The thunder storm's coming so we're taking shelter,
Autumn days are here.

Colin Duncan Brown (11)
Rhu Primary School

AUTUMN

Blackberries are ripening,
Juicy and sweet,
Leaves are falling,
Golden and brown,
Chestnuts are ready,
Shiny and smooth,

Birds are migrating,
A hundred in each flock,
Now it is harvest
And the farmer is busy,
It is autumn
And squirrels hibernate.

There is ice on the road,
It's slippy and cold,
Bonfires are lit,
The wood crackles and snaps,
Now it is autumn,
Summer sleeps.

Gillian Massey (11)
Rhu Primary School

AUTUMN

Autumn is the season when everything changes,
Children playing everywhere,
Red, yellow, brown and golden leaves,
Crispy leaves on the road,
People playing in the leaves,
Everyone is getting ready for Hallowe'en.

Guy Fawkes is burning on his fire,
People watch the fireworks,
Farmers collecting in the harvest,
Squirrels collecting acorns and conkers,
Birds are singing,
Happiness is here.

Christopher Osliff (11)
Rhu Primary School

AUTUMN IS HERE

In autumn the leaves fall from the trees,
The birds begin migrating,
Wonderful yellows, bright reds and oranges,
Guy Fawkes night arrives,
Flames leaping and red hot sparks flying,
Leaves rustling and the wind blowing.

I think autumn is a good time to go outside
And tidy up the garden and prepare for
The spring day by clearing up leaves,
When autumn comes I often light the open fire
In the house and warm my toes,
I love autumn.

Thomas Partridge (11)
Rhu Primary School

CONSERVATION

This smelly gas we're starting to produce,
Has gotta go down, in other words *reduce*,
The solvents and chemicals in wallpaper paste,
It all adds up to far too much waste,

Toxics, car exhausts, CFCs,
The smoke pouring out from the chimneys,
There has to be a way to stop all this pollution,
For all of you P.7s I'll call it a solution.

We've gotta stop damaging the ozone layer,
If we don't stop soon we'll all be out of air,
Our little old planet does not deserve,
All of this pollution so . . .
Please conserve!

Stuart Ackroyd (11)
Rhu Primary School

AUTUMN

The autumn days are growing colder,
My little world is growing older,
Leaves falling silently down,
Turning colours like gold and brown,
Farmers running to fields and back,
Hands full of barley and things like that.

Chestnuts, acorns falling down,
Blocking drains in the town,
Children playing conkers,
Bashing with a thump and a bang,
Migrating birds flying without sleep,
Where will they stop? America, Asia or Greece?

Fire flickering, a burning Guy,
Eating hamburgers, watching sparkler sellers
Walking by,
Everyone is having fun,
Fireworks shooting off in the dark gloomy night,
Oh what a wondrous sight,
Autumn is here again.

Matilda Blick (11)
Rhu Primary School

AUTUMN LEAVES

Autumn leaves start to fall,
Brown, red and gold,
Chills and frosts and fireworks flying,
Birds migrating, chestnuts falling,
Wasps stinging, bells ringing,
Leaves crackling and clocks changing.

Fruit is ready to be picked,
Harvest's here and it's better than ever,
Hay is being gathered in,
Leaves burning in the flames,
Hallowe'en's coming, the Red Devil is singing,
Trick or treaters coming.

Bats flying all night long,
Guys are burning on bonfires,
Chimneys are smoking,
As it gets much colder,
Autumn is here.

Joshua Green (10)
Rhu Primary School

CONSERVATION

Save our planet, stop pollution,
Let's come up with a solution,
Save our wonderful oceans and the fish,
That would be my greatest wish.

Put your rubbish in the bin,
Don't be a litter bug.
You can make a difference if you help,
We deserve a better world.

Save all our wonderful animals,
Beautiful and graceful,
It's up to you to help stop pollution,
You can help!

Save our planet, stop pollution,
Let's come up with a solution.

Cheryl Smith (11)
Rhu Primary School

AUTUMN DAYS

In the autumn fires will burn,
Wind will make the smoke turn,
Leaves flying in the air,
Wind going round my hair,
A leaf flew past me as I turned round,
A baby leaf fell slowly down.

Leaves are falling as they crunch,
Fireworks exploding,
In the autumn leaves will fall down the tree
As it's coming closer to me . . .
Hallowe'en is coming soon,
Masks are going on your face,
Trick or treat, smell my feet
Give me something good to eat.

Amber Howes (11)
Rhu Primary School

AUTUMN

Creeper growing up the wall,
Turning brown by dusky fall,
Squirrels climbing in the trees,
By the waving crispy leaves,
The shiny colours red, gold and brown,
Flash and reflect from the sky to the ground.

Looking forward to fireworks lighting up the sky,
Baking puddings, tarts and pies,
Wrapping up warmly in coats and boots,
Going out into the darkening sky where the owls
Are starting to hoot,
Hallowe'en's visiting the whole of my street,
With sacks full of chocolately treats.

Now the weather is becoming cold and snowy
And the wind is becoming more than blowy,
Presents are being bought
And at school Christmas is being taught,
No one is allowed to be a moaner,
Because Christmas is just around the corner.

Victoria Oswald (10)
Rhu Primary School

AUTUMN

Autumn is a lovely month,
Leaves swirling and twirling from the trees,
With silk inside chestnut shells.

Hallowe'en has come again,
Lit up pumpkins as well,
Children dressed as devils too
And ghosts screaming Eeeeehhhhhooooohhhh.

Crispy golden leaves falling from the trees
And flowers falling from branches,
Fish darting down a stream.

There are also fireworks on Guy Fawkes night,
Red, orange, yellow and blue,
Popping in the sky
And shooting like stars!

Chelsea Sophia Ankorne (11)
Rhu Primary School

BONFIRE NIGHT

Fireworks illuminate the dark sky at night
As children's sparklers flare with might.
Bold, bright colours scorch the sky,
People watch with peering eyes.
Crowds are glaring at the twirling, swirling,
Flames in the sky,
As rockets soar up really high!
They reach their point of blowing up
And crash like cymbals crashing loudly.
Guy Fawkes is burning and making the dark sky bright,
As people watch with joy and delight,
As Guy Fawkes burns out of sight!

William Stolton (11)
Rhu Primary School

FIREWORKS

I watched the rocket
Go up in the sky
And all the colours
Go twinkling by.
The cartwheel zoomed
Off the tree
And hit the Guy
On his knee.

Richard Mulholland (9)
St Andrew's Primary School, Falkirk

FIREWORKS NIGHT

I was grabbing on to my dad's hand with excitement,
Then it was off!
The radiant Roman candle shooting to the heavens,
Then everybody gasped with amazement
At the red Catherine wheel swirling in
The dark, dark night.
The golden sparklers sparkling in my eyes
And silver rockets taking off tonight.

Natalie Ullyart (9)
St Andrew's Primary School, Falkirk

FIREWORKS

As I stood watching
I saw colourful Catherine wheels
Twirling round and round
Then it was the countdown,
10, 9, 8, 7, 6, 5, 4, 3, 2, 1,
Bang!
Blue bangers banging in my ear
Red rockets reaching to the midnight sky,
Silver sparklers sparkling in my eyes,
Then it was all over.
But I was still dizzy
From the colourful Catherine
Wheels twirling round and round.

Jasmine Tshinene (9)
St Andrew's Primary School, Falkirk

FIREWORKS

I stand beside the bonfire watching with delight
As fiery Roman candles light up the night
What a colourful sight.

Rockets go racing by on their journey to the sky
Bright colours catch my eye as they explode - way up high
Oh how I wish I could fly so I could join them in the sky.

The flames from the bonfire begin to get low
I then hear my mum telling me it's time to go
Time for bed David that's the end of the show.

David Harvey (9)
St Andrew's Primary School, Falkirk

FIREWORKS COLOURS NIGHT

Up into the sky
The rockets go
Shooting high
Very, very high,
Bang!
The rockets explode in the dark night
The people standing below
Started to clap and cheer.
At the work of art in the sky,
As colours of the rainbow decorated
The dark night.
A little girl in the crowd,
Holds her mum's hand tightly,
As she watches in amazement,
At the wonderful sight,
In the dark night sky.

Kaitlin Taylor (9)
St Andrew's Primary School, Falkirk

FIREWORKS

It was that night,
I just could not hold my excitement
Then I heard a noise
Boom!
And they're off!
I stood watching the fiery Roman candle,
Dancing in the sky.
I also saw a radiant rocket racing to the stars,
I stood there holding my silvery sparkler
And watching all the colours in the sky.
Then it all stopped
And it seemed as if nothing had happened.

Kevin Gallagher (9)
St Andrew's Primary School, Falkirk

FIREWORKS NIGHT

Through my eyes I see the bonfire burning,
Over on the trees are the Catherine wheels twirling,
Children laughing holding their sparklers sparkling,
I look up at the sky and watch the rockets whizzing,
Oh! What is that noise? It is a banger banging,
Some of the fireworks make it look like lightning,
Suddenly I hear Roman candles fizzing,
Now I am hungry, I'll have one of the sausages sizzling,
The night is so cold and frosty but bright,
Oh! This is a wonderful fireworks night.

Bradley Heeps (9)
St Andrew's Primary School, Falkirk

I Can't Wait!

I can't wait for my birthday,
I want it to come now,
I know which toys I want
A bike, a book, a clown,
I'd really like,
To find my bike,
I'll have a look
for my book,
I'll search up and down
For my clown.
But, no bike, no book
Not even a clown,
All I could find was -
Mum's night-gown!

Emma Guthrie (8)
Shieldhill Primary School

THE MANSION

It's only a mansion
It's only a house
The most scariest thing in there is probably a mouse.

It's only a hall
It's only a place
The things in here disappearing without a trace.

It's only a room
It's only a bedroom
But what is that sheet?

It's only a sheet
It's only a thing
But aaaaaaggghhh! It moved!

Scott Armstrong (9)
Shieldhill Primary School

GREAT BIG LUMP

Sparkle, blutter great big lump.
How I wonder why you're so fat?
Like an elephant you are.
In a flying saucer you live.
You beamed up to your saucer.
You tried to eat me.
I said, 'Eat my children! Eat them! Eat them!
See if I care!'
Great big lump didn't care he just ate me.
Great big lump went to my house and he ate my children.
He said 'Faigsufg! Faigsufg!' - (That means I will take over the world)
He took over the world.

Ross Mercer (9)
Shieldhill Primary School

MY BEST PAL

My best pal is a worm
He wiggles and wiggles
We have worm races
And he crawls on faces.
We have a laugh
On the path or even in the bath at bedtime.
We play with slime
In the morning
It is very boring
And that's my pal.

Declan Ronald (9)
Shieldhill Primary School

SNOW WHITE

There was once a little girl who had a little curl
Who lived with a cruel stepmother
In a small cottage down by the river
With her little doll all shining and red.

Her name was Snow White
When she was six, her mother died,
Her father died when she was nine.

Although the sun was shining
Snow White was still sad
Her garden was lovely and had flowers all over
Bright red roses and daffodils too.

She was so pretty and beautiful too
Her stepmother treated her like a slave
What a wonderful girl she was
So beautiful.

Keri-Anne Reid (9)
Shieldhill Primary School

TOM, TOM THE KING'S SON

Tom, Tom the King's son, he stole a cow, a pig,
A8 duck and a cat and all were eaten and Tom
Got beaten and Tom went howling down the
Street to tell his dad and his mum.

Niall Thomson (9)
Shieldhill Primary School